Beltin'

James Walton

To, Lydia

All tha best !

BENT KEY

Publishing

First published in Great Britain by Bent Key Publishing, 2022
Copyright © James Walton, 2022
The moral right of the author has been asserted.

ISBN: 978-1-915320-02-5

Bent Key Publishing
Owley Wood Road, Weaverham
bentkeypublishing.co.uk

Edited by Rebecca Kenny @ Bent Key
Cover art © Samantha Sanderson-Marshall @ Smash Design and Illustration
smashdesigns.co.uk

Printed in the UK by Mixam UK Ltd.

Typical Northern scruff?
I prefer 'diamond in't rough'

CONTENTS

Beltin'

DAFT AS A BRUSH

Left Turin in floods of tears -
Never saw an English mon as good in years.
A guy distinctive in his Geordie vocabulary:
Always pissed, way past merry.
The same as anyone else blessed wiv two feet,
But he showcased his talent and skill on that Italian neet -

Some said *daft as a brush*,
Others thought his exuberance was way too much
But because of all that, it makes me sad:
To think of the even-better football career he could have had
But he still didn't do too bad
For a local Geordie lad

GRUB

Av got nowt in
Tha spuds are sproutin'
Bread is old
Spattered wi' mold
Chicken is rotten
Slime at tha bottom

I've even checked tha bins -
It's nowt but empty tins
I'll check again just fot mek sure
That me cupboards are deffo empty-bare

No hope of grub
No hope for the pub
I musta pissed off someone who lives above

DOG DAY AFTERNOONS

Wake up wiv a smile an' excitement,
A bowl o'Weetos, mornin' cartoons,
It be time knock for me mates pretty soon.

On came the popper pants, an' tha Reebok classics,
If anyone one 'ad style - I 'ad it.

Make our way t'corna shop,
Nickin' Freddos, Tizer, Dandelion an' Burdock -
Be out all day in't Summer sun,
Lookin' for a chase, we'd play knock-a-door run,

Mucky ears an' durty faces,
Findin' tha greatest wonders in't simplest o'places.

Jumpers f'goalposts,
A scabby owd ball,
Tekkin' free kicks like Becks 'gainst tha wall,
Slidin on't knees,
Then danglin' from trees,
Spend all day on our bikes in tha park,
Be there f'ages, 'til it went dark

When a fink back now,
It kinda meks me sad -
Was some ov tha best times I'd ever really 'ad.

BOOZE, SHAGS AN' KEBABS

Friday's me fave neet o'week,
On't pull in Wigan town, down't famous King street

Quiff up me 'air wi' a big tub o'wet look gel,
Douse me pits an' clothes in Lynx Africa to mask tha smell

Get tanked up on cheap ale an' shots in't local pub,
Then 'ead out early t'get in't clubs

Girls in't tight dresses and big 'eels,
All they ad do w'skip a few meals

Lads wi' tans and super-tight shirts,
Its inevitable - they'll all get skirt

That's if they dunt get in a scrap -
All macho bullshit; I 'ate that crap

I stand all pale, loaded up on ale,
So drunk, am surprised I lived to tell't tale

T'slightly sober up on donner meyt an chips,
Tha garlic mayo coatin' me lips

All I want from't neet is a world-class shag
An' what I end up with is a piss-poor ten bag

So good night, God bless.
I need me rest
From tha sesh.

DIG OUT YA DOLE

Signin on't dole
Teks piss out ya soul
Brass that's lent
Won't cover tha rent
Real bad news
Ya need scavenge f'food

Forget gas an' leccy
No chance f'brekkie
Shoes av 'oles
Rips and tears in ya clothes
Real bad news
No money for booze

Anuv'ver serious issue
Th'expensive price of decent toilet tissue
A freezin-cowd shower
Leavin ya fert shiver an' cower
Tha real bad news -
It worsens ya blues

But I ain't got a choice but t'get ont dole,
I'll just av t'settle wiv a few quid for me soul.

DISCO 99

Once a year we 'ad a school disco in't assembly 'all
Ya paid a quid f'get in
Then began t'free f'all

Girls on one side
Boys on t'over
All neet long
They wunt speyk t'one anuvver

Lasses fot first time in make-up an' jewellery
Lads in trackies, up to tomfoolery

Me fave bit was tuck shop an' hot dogs
Pick an' mix an' fizzy pop

A sin a kid eat that much he threw up in't bogs

Sat wi ya pals as they blasted out Spice Girls
Some lasses doin' splits,
Uvvers doin' twirls

We wud sit an' just do nowt -
But when they played Eiffel 65
We'd slide on't knees an' dive about

By end o'neet we'd be smacked-up on sugar
Collected by angry parents
Unimpressed wiv our clothes
Scuffed t'bugger

GALLOWAYS

Ya can't beyt a Galloways pie
Me final meal before I die -
Butter an' onion, meyt an' tater
Av one now, save ova f'later
This pastry could av added charm
Tek one 'ome, try it on a barm
A Wigan delight t'highlight ov ya day
Tasty samples of a beige buffet
1971 was tha start of Galloways bakers
Nowadays
They are Wigan's dream makers

ONE OV A MILLION

Always an early riser -
Automatic, body clock rings out at 5am
Too early t'stomach any brekkie;
A cup o'black coffee is all't nutrition he needs
Dunk is 'ed in freezin' water
His birth certificate claims him t'still be a young un
But the wrinkles an' scars, ache of his bones sez ovvawise
Ridin t'work in a van half his age,
Splutters out diesel-flavoured smoke
That compliments tha early mornin' sky,
Tha vehicle skips an' jumps all tha way t'nearest demolition site
Workin' skin t'bone
He stands and works, sufferin' agony alone
When he can finally stomach tha food,
It's fatty, greasy, un-nutritious and sickenin'
But it's all he can afford
Bloodied knuckles and plucked fingernails
Bear no contest to the pain he suffers at tha end of every day.
Back in the van, he tries t'sleep,
His carcass lies in defeat
Nothin' it can do but weep -
Back home alone, a silent phone, repeats on't telly;
His dinner is the only meal he can tolerate
Of the liquid variety. He feeds his thirst, shelters the agony
Ov all the hurt etched into his skin,
It is no match f'the demons within.
He's worked 'ard all his life
He 'as no kids, he 'as no wife
Many found it 'ard
Not even enough brass to afford a house with a yard
Every day - same as tha next,

Burnin' in his lower back worse than before
His body is screamin out f'him t'give in
He dunt know why, but he can't.
Voices inside tell 'im that's not what's expected
Ya must carry on. Do ya bit.
Tha's plenty time t'think an rest when ya dead

AFTERNOON AT THA GEE-GEES

I neva thought it all that
A booze-soaked weekend f'common twat

Lasses out int' short-short-dresses
LadsladsLADS arrive in masses

S'much fake tan
Twice as much on every man

At tha behest of tha horse
Bookies offer fortunes t'change ya life
No more strugglin, no more strife

Tha 'orse falls, it must be shot
But ya cunt give a toss coz ya lost tha lot

But now: tha real fun begins
Fags, drugs an' all kinda sins

Prosecco an' pints
Spewin' up an' fights

Hair extensions torn out
Beer-bellied blokes out f'count

It all became a scene reminiscent ov that Hills Av Eyes

Tha horses seemed more civilised

AWAY DAYS

All aboard tha number 72
Me, me nan an' me grandad
Buzzin f'our day in Blackpool

Vegas o'North!

Tha nostalgia ov tha sea, tha arcades,
Toffee rock an' tha tower
Nan an' Grandad devour tha fave dish:
Fish, chips an' mushy peys

I wa' less romantic an' stuffed me face wi' sugared doughnuts

On't 2p machines I work multiple slots at a time,
Burnin' off tha sugar
Me nan toppin' up me brass once I got t'me last few

After hours o'play I collected me winnins
7 quid in coppers t'spend at Woolworths

Before we got on't bus 'ome
We'd tek walk down North Pier
I'd be out in front, ice cream all round me chops

Nan an' Grandad 'oldin 'ands like it was their first date
Av ad tha best day ov me life

Lookin' back at me nan an' me grandad,
I can tell they've ad a beltin' day too

ME, MESELF AN' A BEER

The first time in seven years I've spent it alone.
Nobody with me -
Nobody at the end of the phone.
I'm not usually one for sentimental shite
Especially on fuckin' Valentine's night -
This time, I try an' find someone new
I think I've found it - in a beer or two
It never criticises or makes a sigh
It's by my side as I bubble and cry
I used to fuckin' hate me, meself an' I -
I could be one of the many that would take that choice to die,
But talking with me old friend here
(Ya know, tha beer -)
I guess I've found something to live for.
Oh so clear, in a drunken haze
Forgetting many a dour day
For when I'm feeling down
It keeps me around
So pour another round!

It's what keeps me here.
Just me, meself, an' a beer.

BOG ROLL

Cushioned layers enriched with lotion,
Soft and fragranced, for every bowel motion

Always follow this strict routine,
It's damn sure to keep your bum 'ole clean

Must always wipe from front-to-back,
When cleanin' up your dirty arse-crack

Use enough roll to make a boxing glove on your fist,
Make sure there's plenty so tha's not covered in shit

Once the mess is cleared,
Use one last layer to make sure it's all disappeared

Pull up your kecks and check on your poo,
Then it's all good to flush on down the loo

Now to initiate the final demands,
Is to lather up tha soap and wash those 'ands.

SAT'DAY NEET

When you sit in that hot Madagascan sun
Skin favver's a Drumstick lolly
Plenty of tinnies
Tons of music
I feel especially
Fuckin' down
But I know
That when the footie or ruggers returns
I'll feel decent again, man.
When I can get me Gazelles out from tha box
Me best Fred Perry an' tha best Owd Spice for me chops
I've got me season ticket
Ready an' waiting.
Just t'see tha lads again - tha lads I've known for s'many years
Meet up in tha boozer
Share a pint or ten -
Enter the holy grail of Sat'day afternoons
T'stand wi' thousand other locals,
Passionate an' die-hard.
Even if tha game goes arse-over-tit
We shall stand strong -
What was once a few blokes cheering their town
Is now a place for the whole family
When't game is over
We despair or cheer wiv each other
Whether a sister or a brother
We all leave the holy grail as one
Through each town or city
It might not mean summert t'you
But it'll deffo mean summert t'me
Cos when Sat'day comes
Tha's no place I'd rather be

CHIPPY TAY

Busiest neet o'week f'Mr. Bradbury's fish supper bar.
Folk queuing round the bend and further than Pepper Lane
As far as I can si'thee.
Entering the Holy Grail of fried delicacies,
Mounds of chips are chucked in't fryer;
Old mon Dicky Sykes scoffs his pey wet and chips,
I'm that clempt I order two small smacks
Just whilst I wait for me end-of-wik treat.

I make me order of fish and chips -
Mek it large cos I ain't driving.
Tons of salt, tons of vinegar an' a generous helping
Of mushy peys.
Sprinkled across is a lovely layer of scraps and
T'top it all off, a can of Irn Bru and a Dandelion & Burdock.
Less than a tenner, all in.
Even got enough left over for a couple wooden forks an' a
Pudding, peas an' gravy for me mam.

Beltin'.

TELLY LICENSE

I don't bother with the telly licence me,
There's never owt on it to really see,
Especially since they fucked off BBC Three -
Kids these days get more from an on-demand service,
Not a channel that no longer showcases
The talents of Peter Purves -
It used be free,
When you was an age like seventy-three;
The Goon Squad listen round the corner
Via their detector-car transmissions -
The bully-boys come banging at the doors of senior citizens,
Asking for money or the threat of a court summons,
Tell 'em to do one.
Ya don't scare me.
I'm not 'ere to pay for the expenses of the Commissioner Chief,
After all, he's tha one that's the thief,
So I'll tek that writ
But only
'Coz I need a shit

FRIDAY NEET AT THA TAKEY

Am 'ungry, need food but a can't be arsed go shop t'day
Instead al g'down t'local takeaway

Tha Cluckin' Cottage is like a shinin' beam
From Southern-fried t' thi'talian cuisine

Munchin on't chicken wings
Only 12% poultry. Rest made up ov unidentifiable things

Greasy lips
From cheesy chips
Take C off it, what'dya ya get?

'ips

Then in't mornin, feelin tha ick
Ya tummy grumbles
Begin feelin' sick
Arse'ole mumbles...

But in't end its all worth the risks
Be strapped t'bog

Wi' squits

SCHOOL DINNERS

When tha bell rang, we'd race out tha class room
And up tha squeaky corridor floor,

Wanted t'be tha first t'get in tha dinner hall
And find out what's in store

We'd line up like it's a military parade
Find out if our lunch dreams had been made

Beans, chips or Smiley Faces,
Essential to ya diet, a delight t'taste it,

And tha greatest thing they could give ya:
A Bernard Matthews' Turkey Twizzler.

But tha best thing t'touch me 'art
Was a sprinkle cake, pink custard an'
A golden cornflake tart.

BEST DRINK O' DAY

Ow d'ya mek tha best drink o'day?
Ask most people, they'll 'av a different say
Some put tha milk in before tha 'ot watter
Others would argue on this triflin' matter

I tek a Yorkshire tea bag, chuck it in me fave mug
Leave it in a while,
Let tha fing brew
But never let it stew.

Top it off wi' milk, just a couple o'drops
Wen mekkin a brew, ya pull out all tha stops

And if I think you're tha same as me -
I tek two sugars in me tea

SUNDAY LEAGUE

Arise 'ungover
30 minutes before kick off
Gaffer's gonna av me guts f'garters
In a rush, I pull on me mis-matched footie socks
A pair o'short-shorts from tha Kevin Keegan era

Before a'pack me tatty boots an' placcy shinnies
I throw up last night's festivities into t'bog
A gentle but painful jog t'the pitch leaves me gaspin f'air.

Tha gaffer's mad, but at least I turned up -
He gives us tha team talk t'not be a bunch o'soft arses
An' get stuck in

Tha bog is blocked wiv four pounds of log and
The showers are even worse
So I tek a wiz in a bush outside

Smoke a fag f'those much-needed vitamins
Swig a full bottle o'Lucozade

I cross the white line
Greb on the holy turf
I'm all set for a game o'football -
Just a typical Sunday mornin'.

VAMPIRES

Never set foot in't town or city
No willingness t'invest in't transfer kitty
Suckin' up all tha club's profits
Its die-ard fans fight 'eaven an 'ell t'stop it
Sellin' off every single asset, piece-by-piece
Til t'club has nowt -
Its existence will cease;
So-called governin' bodies incite rules fo't greater good
But do sod-all when these vampires suck on the blood
Of every single club
Leavin' em penniless an broke -

They'll leave in a hurry.

Just look what happened
T'clubs like Bury.

LIFE IN'T LEAGUE

Let me set tha scene
F'game o'rugby league
It's bred into ya blood - tha community
In its towns an cities, developin' that unity
Fans would come t'gevver at grounds like Central Park
These days, they watch analysis by lads like Phil Clarke

As brothers in arms on tha field
Fightin f'one anuvver - they do not yield

Blood, sweat and tears.
Every player, challengin' their fears
Cheered on by't crowd;
Those thirteen players makin'em proud -

On and off tha field they can be 'eroes
Just like Mike Gregory and Rob Burrow
Entwined in its 'eritage;
Forever in ya history -

Always part of ya club.

Tha first 125 years 'av gone so well
It all began in a Huddersfield hotel
So ere's t'many years more
Ov tha greatest sport t'hit our shore

CHRISTMAS DISEASE

December 25th an' tha awkward festivities wi' those
Ya 'opefully neva see but once a year

Generosity ov gifts ya don't need
Frowns when ya clearly ain't spent as much
On their unwanted prezzie

Neva t'realise ya bought these items
Wiv a few bob ya pulled 'gevver

But that's not all -

Tha family conversation at Christmas gives ya more indigestion
Than ya traditional dry turkey dinner -
Spanish inquisition on ya non-existent love life,
Mundane workin' wik, an how ya manage to get thru
Livin t'way ya do -
Cousin Steve brags 'bout his new Mercedes and
Pullin' in a three-figure salary
But he dunt gloat

All whilst bein forced t'eat tha same Christmas cake as every year
Each moutful tastin' worse than tha last -

Snowballs, Buck's Fizz, or any form of free ale
Tha only savin' grace when ya av t'play charades
Wiv a pissed-up auntie and a touchy-feely uncle
Who's afta every young lass at tha party

These days
I feel once a year is gettin t'much

BISCUIT TIN

When I go me nan's, she sez
"Ya 'ands always in that ruddy biscuit tin!
   Goodness sake Jim, keep 'aytin an tha won't stay slim."
Triples, Penguins, Golds and Taxis
S'many t'choose - al aft 'av one ov each!

I guess it meks sense me backside's a big oval peach
What can I say, I can't keep away -
Always summert in me gob

A digestive or a chocolate 'ob nob

BACK IN'T SCHOOL DAYS

A load ov me mates sed they'd love g'back,
Must'a liked avin their undies pult up their arse-crack,
'Ours an 'ours ov maths ad bloody 'ate,
All tha numbers an decimals would just mek me procrastinate.
Neet after neet ov 'orrible detention,
All cos I 'ad me own ideas a dared t'mention,
I wa' always tha year's class clown.
Wuz tha perfect mask t'keep me frum feelin down -
Teachers tell ya that ya need ya life sorted out;
Am aged 30. Nah. I still 'av no idea what life's about,
Ya wanna feel alive?
Do what ya enjoy. Strive -
Strive t'make a change -
N'matter if ovas find it teeterin on strange
Dunt listen t'them cunts on what t'do
Follow ya dreams -
You do you

PROCESSED MEYTS AN' SUGARY SWEETS

Processed meyts an sugary sweets
On't telly are *Neighbours* repeats

A lovely sweet brew in ya fave Jelly Babies mug
Way back when sugar wasn't treated like an illegal drug

This wa' back int' day when we 'ad bulky TV sets
Un'all me collection o'films wa' recorded on VHS cassettes

When family time wa' quality time
An sittin in front ov a screen weren't seen as a crime

'MEMBER WHEN..?

'Member wen Coca-Cola used't taste like proper coke?
Plenty o' sugar t'give ya that all-day buzz,
When blue Smarties 'ad enough e-numbers
T'replace the entire alphabet wit letter E,
If ya drank so much Sunny D
It gave ya skin a David Dickinson vibe?

Wen tha was such a fing called a penny sweet
That cost just that?
Now it's a penny sweet at ten pence apiece.
A 50p pick-a-mix would be that exact value,
2020 - and it's 50p for 20p's worth,
They introduced a sugar tax,
But they still ain't what they used be -
So what am I payin' f'?

It dunt matter anyway,
I'm diabetic,
I can't really have any of that stuff any more.

BEST MEAL O' DAY

First fings first, get a decent-tastin meat an'tater pie.

Second.
Slice a fluffy, white, barmcake in 'alf
An cover wi'loadsa butter.

Third.
Tek ya pie out o'tray an place it on't bottom 'alf o'tha barmcake.
Place tha top 'alf on but mek sure ya don't mek a bloody mess.

Fourth.
Tha best bit.

Eat.

ACKNOWLEDGEMENTS

Thanks to:

Galloways fot beltin' jackbit

Sir Ben Watson for that goal at Wembley on't 11th May 2013

All me pals

Me family

People o'Wiggin

Me Nan and Grandad Walton f'elpin' me create memories that a could write 'bout

Every creative that dunt av a pot piss in

ABOUT THE AUTHOR

James Walton is a writer born and bred in Wigan.

His Northern roots heavily influence his writing style and various screenplays, stories and poems.

He chooses to write phonetically to show that good writing isn't all about grammar and punctuation - it's also about heart and soul.

ABOUT BENT KEY

It started with a key.

Bent Key is named after the bent front-door key that Rebecca Kenny found in her pocket after arriving home from hospital following her car crash. It is a symbol - of change, new starts, risk and taking a chance on the unknown.

Bent Key is a micropublisher with ethics. We do not charge for submissions, we do not charge to publish and we make space for writers who may struggle to access traditional publishing houses, specifically writers who are neuro-divergent or otherwise marginalised. We never ask anyone to write for free, and we like to champion authentic voices.

All of our beautiful covers are designed by our graphic designer Sam at SMASH Illustration, a graphic design company based in Southport, Merseyside.

Find us online:
bentkeypublishing.co.uk

Instagram/Facebook   @bentkeypublishing
Twitter   @bentkeypublish